Conversation with a Millionaire Real Estate Investor

Conversation with a Millionaire Real Estate Investor

Brant Phillips

Ainsley&Allen
PUBLISHING

Ainsley & Allen Publishing LLC
2035 Sunset Lake Road
Newark, DE 19702
www.ainsleyallenpublishing.com

ISBN-10: 1-946694-01-0
ISBN-13: 978-1-946694-01-0

CONTENTS

PROLOGUE

Before we get started, let me first disclose that my mentor's name has been changed to protect his identity. He does not seek fame, publicity, or recognition for this work, but he does share the same desire as I do to educate and inspire others to take action. Nothing else in this book has been altered out of context.

Brace yourself. You are about to witness first-hand what perhaps no other real estate book has done before. I am going to take you behind closed doors to witness a conversation between myself and one of my mentors that will reveal to you the mindset of successful real estate entrepreneurs. You'll learn how my mentor has accumulated a massive net worth after starting from a humble beginning mopping floors and cleaning toilets.

I promise you this book is a no B.S. approach to business and is 100% REAL and TRANSPARENT about what it takes to create wealth and succeed in today's market. It is my mission to motivate, educate, inspire, and equip you to begin taking massive action in your real estate investments. I've done my part, now it's up to you.

INTRODUCTION

Over the years, I've been fortunate to have some really tremendous people in my life that have helped me carve out my niche in the sometimes-crazy world of being an entrepreneur. I can't say enough about my friends and family, especially my wife and all of the support she's given me. I've also had some incredible mentors that have helped me along the way.

Several years ago, I was fortunate to meet James, who is the focus of this book. He has experienced incredible success in real estate, business and life, and has accomplished many of the outcomes in his business that I'm seeking to replicate in mine.

James is 65 years young and has created a massive net worth through real estate investing in multi-family and commercial industries, but he's also owned hotels and a variety of other types of real estate. He now focuses his efforts on private lending and loans money to investors who are out doing deals. And, by the way, he runs seven miles per day.

For those of you that know me, or have heard me speak, or read any of my books or blog posts, you know that I'm a big advocate of seeking guidance or mentorship when venturing into new arenas. Sure, you can do it alone, but as I see so often, the road alone is much longer and far more difficult to navigate.

Good guidance and mentorship typically can do two things:

1. Speed up results; and
2. Help you avoid many of the pitfalls that are on the road you're traveling.

Mentors will provide encouragement and support when you need it most. So, this is my focus of the book. I want you to hear from one of my mentors how he accumulated wealth many times over. He started out like so many of us do: broke and at the bottom. He used to clean toilets many years ago, and now he has created a massive financial empire and an incredible life. Just as important, James's energy and personality are both electric and contagious. I consider it an honor to know this man, to be able to call him a mentor, and to share his wisdom with you now.

This book begins mid-conversation with me telling James about the last corporate job I held before deciding to become a real estate investor and entrepreneur. Enjoy!

PART I – CONVERSATION

After seven years on the police force, I decided to try something else. I reached a point where I couldn't take the police department politics and I knew 100 percent that I was done so I got a job, and I hated it from the first day.

I thought I would find a good company to work for and climb the corporate ladder. I remember coming home from my very first day on the job, and my wife asked, "How was it?" I calmly and clearly replied, "I absolutely hate it but I'm going to do it, and I'm going to do it well. So, don't worry about our finances, but I'm getting out as soon as I can. I'm going to figure out how to do that, but I have no idea what that is right now."

It was a corporate sales job, and there were so many aspects of the job I didn't like, such as wearing a suit and tie, the corporate speak, having a boss, and having to complete all of these stupid reports. I would ask my boss quite frequently, "Can't I just make you more money and not do all this nonessential stuff?" "No, you have to do all this stuff," was, of course, the response. So, I was a good little corporate boy and finished number one or number two in sales every year I worked there. In hindsight, I realize that job helped fuel the motivation that led me to be an entrepreneur in real estate and everything else I do now. So, now, here we are.

I get it. You're preaching to the choir. I always feel bad for the people that are not honest with themselves like you were.

When you are not honest with yourself or are afraid, fear will control you if you allow it...and we all have fears. Myself included. If we allow fear to run our lives, we end up not being very happy. Fighting the fears can be a challenge at times.

One of my mentors always talks about how what we want exists on the other side of our fear. What we want is right there in front of us, so to speak, but we have to go through this "fear/space" to get there. A lot of people will touch it, put their finger on it, and say, "Oh that hurts!" and they'll turn around, but what they really want is on the other side of that "pain," or on the other side of our fear.

When I started in real estate; I was still working my job, and began buying houses on the side. I was working two jobs because I was buying a house almost every month when I first started in real estate.

One day I was talking with my boss—whom I had a really good relationship with—about real estate. I told her what I was doing after I bought a couple of rental houses, and she said, "That's really cool. Keep me informed on how that goes. I've always wanted to try that." After I bought about four or five houses in as many months, I stopped telling her because I didn't want her to know how aggressively I was pursuing my investing business and preparing to leave my job.

I wasn't slacking at my job during this time. I was finishing number one or number two every year in sales, so I don't think she really cared as long as I was hitting my numbers. Still, my thought was that it would be best to keep my investing pursuits to myself.

During the first year at my job, I was telling a coworker of mine, John, that I was starting in real estate. He said, "Man, I've always wanted to do that. I've always wanted to do that," over and over, every time we would talk about real estate. Eventually, I stopped telling him about my investments as well. Every now and then when we were talking, he would say, "How is your real estate doing?" I would tell him, "It's doing great. It's a lot of work, but it's doing great." His response was typically, "Well, my wife won't let me do it. My wife won't let me do it." Basically, John was making excuses rather than finding solutions and taking action.

When I was leaving the company two and a half years later, I bumped into John, and he still hadn't done a deal. I had about 25 rental properties that I had purchased during that time. When he asked me why I was leaving the company, I told him I was going to focus on real estate full-time. His jaw dropped when I told him I had 25 properties because the last time we had talked about real estate, I was only at five or six.

I met with my boss for a review on the same day I decided to leave the company, and there was an awards banquet scheduled for the following week. I was going to receive an award, and I was also going to be offered a promotion. At the end of my review, she said, "Is there anything you want to tell me?" My response was, "Yes, I won't be at the awards banquet, and I'm putting in my two weeks' notice and leaving the company to focus on real estate." Her first response was classic. She said, "Damn. Can you teach me how to do it so I can leave too?" We both had a great laugh, and I did help her do some real estate. I coached her and her husband a little, and they ended up doing five or six deals over the next couple of years.

Now back to the topic of fear. That day she talked about her fear of pursuing something outside the "safety" of the corporate world. I would say fear is one of the biggest things that I see that people allow to limit their success. The funny thing is, most times, the fear that we create in our minds isn't even anything that we actually experience.

Often, when we actually experience a "bad" situation, we realize it's actually not that bad. Honestly, that's how I've learned my greatest lessons as an entrepreneur, by going through things that scared me a little bit and were a little painful. The bottom line is, even when

I've gotten hurt in business, I've learned the most and it's made me stronger.

But, don't you think fear is created by outside influences as well? When you think about your childhood, does anything pop up in your mind, where you find yourself placing blame on someone for putting 'the fear of God' in you when you were a child that you're still battling with today? Who was that person for you?

For me, it was my father. He always had a corporate job and feared leaving that comfort zone. He tried to persuade me to follow a similar path.

For me, it was my mother. It's like she was afraid of her own shadow.

They were either afraid or comfortable and thought that the job was their security. I think the only security any person has is themselves. It's not the corporate company, because they don't care about you. It's very simple: If you stop performing, what security do you have there? Nothing, you're out. If you can perform there, the question is, "Why can't you perform on your own?"

Let's be realistic because there are some people that need leadership and guidance all their lives, but on your own, you can get that. You can rent it; you can pay for it. You don't have to work for it. They can work for you, and you can accomplish the same goal, but a lot of people just don't realize that. In addition to fear, I think they aren't really ready to make the sacrifices.

You've made a lot of sacrifices in as many years as you've been building your portfolio and businesses and being on your own. You weren't at the bar every night. You might have been drinking, but you weren't at the bar every night, and you didn't have as much time to play. How can you? When you're working two jobs, your business and someone else's. I've been there. I had a lot of things going on too when I was a young guy starting out.

Tell us a little about your background. Where did you start and what ultimately led you to real estate?

It goes back to when I was young and watching my parents, similar to yours, working for someone else and struggling financially. Every week when my dad came home with his paycheck, and I heard it, and it upset me big time. I think that stuck with me. I said, that's not going to be me. I don't know how, but I'm going to figure out how. I'm going to be the guy he works for and make a bunch of money. That was the beginning for me, I would say.

Growing up, I became very motivated to make money. Basically, I wanted the finer things in life, which my parents didn't have. Before I was a teenager—and while I was a teenager and my friends were out partying—I would find odd jobs to make money, even cleaning toilets. When my friends were on vacation during the Christmas holidays or summer break, I found a job, and it didn't matter what type of job. They weren't pretty jobs, but I didn't care, because I was making money.

When we were kids going out on dates before we could drive, my friends took their dates out on the bus, but I took my dates out in a taxi. Life was good. I went to a finer restaurant; they went to MacDonald's. When we went on trips as kids, they stayed at the YMCA, and I stayed in a nice hotel. That really became very important to me.

 Hearing you talk about how your influences started at a very young age reminds me of my childhood and how it has impacted me. I'll bet this is the same for others.

When I was growing up, we struggled a lot financially. I will also say that I had a really great childhood, so it's not all rain clouds and teary eyes, but there was a period of time when I was 12-13 years old and my father lost his job for almost two years. He was affected by the oil and gas industry, and we eventually lost our house. My parents filed bankruptcy. We were dead broke for several years, and it was tough. I remember seeing the look of pain and struggle in my parents' eyes and knew that I didn't want to experience that again, nor did I want my kids to go through that.

My best friend's dad was an entrepreneur. He had a construction business, and did some real estate investing as well along with some rental properties. I'd spend the night with my friend on Fridays and his dad would take us to work with him early the next morning. We'd get breakfast from Jack in the Box and go walk around houses and look at projects.

Eventually, my dad found work in Houston and we moved from Dallas. I had to leave all of my childhood friends. I remember that to this day, and I think it still drives me. The lesson I learned from my father was corporate America will not provide safety and security, because at the drop of a hat, you can be gone.

I know some people are more geared toward being employed, and there's nothing wrong with that, but I knew it wasn't for me. I wanted to have the ability to provide for my family no matter what. When I left the corporate world, my father said, "What are you doing leaving a good job with a Fortune 500 company?"

He didn't understand that the corporate life wasn't for me. He saw what I was doing as risky, but spending the next 20 or 30 years of my life in corporate America seemed much riskier than doing and pursuing what excited me, even if it meant setbacks. Fortunately, I haven't had major setbacks and I've done very well, but it would have been okay if setbacks happened, and I was very willing to take on those risks. I was driven by what happened in my childhood and wanted to have a better life. In hindsight, I'm incredibly thankful for the difficult times that I've experienced.

We are molded from those experiences for sure, but I think always as we move forward in life and in our businesses—I was going to say careers, but I don't think that we have careers. I'd like to say career, because it sounds better, but we have businesses.

We're both wearing shorts and sneakers. This isn't corporate attire. I just met with some bankers dressed like this, and that's what I always do, because this is how I dress. I'll make an excuse when I meet with them, like, "Oh, I was just at a property...." Being dressed like this and living like this is one of the perks of our sacrifices and our successes, but what you also find is this: Fear is there. You can't ignore it because it's not going away. You have to constantly overcome it, even to this day, even at my age. You have to never forget.

Actually, I'll tell you who kind of says this quite a bit. I watch the show *Shark Tank* so I have respect for most of the people on there. One of the guys that I think is the shrewdest—forget Mr. Wonderful. He's a brilliant guy, and his money made him even smarter, because he scored big, right? But Mark Cuban, there is a guy that appears to be shrewder than all the rest of them. One of the things he preaches, or at least my interpretation is, that no matter how much money you have, no matter how successful you are, when you get up in the morning, you have to tackle that day as if it were your first tackle, and you had to make that first dollar all over again, because as soon as you get soft, you start to lose it again.

He refreshed me on that, because every once in a while, we need a refresher. There's someone who came into my life in around 2009 and has stayed in my life till now, who has taught me not to be lazy. Obviously, I'm not lazy or I wouldn't be successful, but what I mean by lazy is that sometimes we tend to procrastinate. I don't know if you have that problem, but I think a lot of people do.

The problem is I could do that tomorrow. Maybe I won't get in the car and drive to Dallas today and come back this afternoon; I'll wait and I'll see the guy another time. You can't procrastinate. You've got to stop yourself and say, "Hey, I'm a doer, and I've got something that has to get done. I'm not going to let procrastination get in the way." There's more than fear that we're battling; there's also procrastination and a little bit of laziness.

In today's high-tech world, we're texting; we're emailing; we're talking on the phone—and that's all good. There's nothing wrong with it and most times it can be productive, but you can't beat face-to-face interactions. We can't forget that. There's nothing like being able to read the body language, do the eyeball test, and make that deal or not make that deal. How can you judge a person by a text or an email? You can't know what they're really thinking by a text or an email or even on the phone. You've got to be together in person.

You've got to push yourself, I believe, to have face time with people. Face time with people not only gets you further ahead, but you also learn from it. You'll learn more from a person when you're sitting across from them than you do when you're using any other means of communication. Now, that's my personal belief. I'm not against texting, emailing, and telephone calls. I'm not old-fashioned, because I text. I email. I do everything that all the Millennials do.

I believe that there are certain things that don't change, and there are things that do, and face time will never change. That's why the President has his own jet, and he travels all over the world. He could pick up a phone, send texts and email too. Why is he hopping on a plane and going to visit people all over the world? Because you can't make a deal otherwise. You can't develop a relationship. If you can't develop a relationship, how do you make a good deal?

Your network is your net worth. What you said about laziness is important. Life's a game and there is a point where business becomes a game too. I've seen a lot of people in business get to the point where they are successful, but then their laziness sets in. I've also seen people who are only on their second or third real estate deal become lazy, or they "let their guard down," so to speak.

Maybe their first deal went really well because they were focused, but because it went so well, they lose their edge and begin to get lazy and cut some corners. Then, on their second deal, they get the sophomore slump and they fail to use discipline.

That's a word I've heard you emphasize before and that learning to say no is one of the most important disciplines to have.

I believe it is, and it's not just saying no. It's really saying, "I have a proven formula." I do have a proven formula that works for me, just like you have your own...but everybody's formula is different. Is it perfect? No, nobody's formula is perfect. We all make mistakes, but my formula has been successful enough that I can stay in the game and continue to get ahead. We can never forget that proven formula. That's what happens to some people—as soon as they have some success, they forget where they came from.

Some people develop an attitude and think they're "holier than thou." Some people end up fooling themselves and changing their formula and forgetting the discipline, forgetting the formula that got them there. But the investor that continues to be successful is the one that has his antennae up all the time, because the world is constantly changing around us, and he has to change. He or she has to change their formula with it and continue to maintain the discipline or, in simple terms never take off the armor. You can meet people, if you let these things go to your head, and let your heart take over and drop the armor and the discipline, you lose the money.

You can be the nicest individual, and there's no reason why you shouldn't walk around with a smile every day, and when you meet people that you're going to do business with, have a great time and build a relationship. When it comes time to make a decision, a proposal, or an offer, you have to be prepared to draw the line no matter what, because you know if you cross that line, it's not going to work for you. You know from experience, as do I. But it's not natural to be able to easily tell someone no once you like someone and you're talking to them.

You want to help them—that's the natural side of every human being. This is where the discipline and the training comes in. You can and should be able to do it with a smile. Never be afraid to tell people exactly like it is and not waste their time. The people that upset me the most are the people that don't tell me the truth right away. Does that make sense? In other words, listen, if my deal isn't going to work for you, tell me.

You can tell me, "I don't know if I can do it, but let me look around. If I can't do better, I'll be back to you." Be honest. I try to do the same thing. It's important not to waste people's time. If you go look at a deal, and you don't like it, be upfront. Say, "Call me on the next one. I don't like this location. I'm not touching it for 10 cents." What's so wrong about that?

We're in an election year now. We have two candidates: Donald Trump and Hillary Clinton. If you take Trump out of the race and just put him in business, he's your kind of guy, because he'll tell you right to your face exactly where he stands. You may not like it, but that's not important. It's not a question of liking. You want to know where the person across from you stands. Your typical politician will never tell you. They'll just bulls@#t you all the way with sweet talk. You've seen it; I've seen it. I'm not discussing here whom we're voting for; I'm just saying what kind of people we should be when it comes to relationships and doing business.

Now, Trump is a little rough around the edges. I think he could be a little more polished, but he is who he is. You hear closer to what he's thinking than you hear from your typical politician. When he's talking, he doesn't always have all the answers. I guess that's his right if he's in business, and he's running the business and he owns it, but I think that's extremely important to be very decisive, because there's no magic to what we do, is there?

I tell people all the time that business is not that difficult. It's just doing the little things every single day, picking up the phone, going to meetings, looking at new deals. And a lot of people think the numbers and the math are difficult, but they are not.

The math is easy. I tell people all the time, "If I can do this, you can do this. It's just a matter of rolling up your sleeves and doing the work."

Do you have a college degree?

I have a degree in Criminal Justice. After high school, I did not plan to go to college. I was going to just get a job. Quite frankly, I had a hard time graduating high school. I moved back to Dallas with one of my childhood friends, and we got jobs at a warehouse loading trucks, I did that for about six months and decided I didn't want to do that forever. The work was rough and low-paying, of course, so that's when I decided to go to college.

I did that type of work too. You don't need a degree to do what we do in our business. It helps to be mathematically inclined to a certain degree. I don't know how to operate a spreadsheet, but I can read a financial statement, and that's what really matters. I didn't go to college, but I can read a financial statement because it's really simple. When I do deals, I take my iPhone and my calculator on my iPhone, and I figure it out. Maybe I take a piece of paper and a pen once in a while, but normally I use my iPad.

I think that what we do is like an acquired taste. Over time, it's like drinking wine. Over time, you get better at it and better at it, and you enjoy it more and more as you do it.

Recently, one of my students from out of town came to Houston to look at properties with us during a coaching/ training day. He had gone under contract on his first deal right before coming down. Before he went under contract, there was a lot of back and forth between us—phone calls, emails, texts, what about this and what about that? He sent me spreadsheets and was doing exactly what I've taught him to do, and that's what he's supposed to do, I'm his real estate coach after all.

Anyways, during our training day, we went to a property that we had already bought and closed on. My project manager was there along with our contractors starting the renovations. I had not seen the house before that day. My student was surprised at that. Then, we went to another house that I was scheduled to close on the next day, and I hadn't seen that house before either. The last house we went to was a new deal and another investor was there looking at it as well, so I knew we had some competition, as we always do. I pulled out my phone, ran some numbers, and then had one of my partners review the numbers. About five minutes later, I said, "Let's do it." My student asked, "That's it?" That's really the way it is for us on a lot of single-family homes we do. No, they aren't all this simple, but after time, the game just speeds up and gets much, much easier.

It takes a little longer in the beginning. You've got to do more homework, but once you get the knack, you can do your due diligence and know where you stand. I will tell you, personally, I don't do any deal unless I eyeball it myself.

I agree. I've only bought a few houses sight unseen, but I have a full-time buyer, and that's all he does. I see pictures, videos, etc. All of the houses I have bought sight unseen have been typical "bread and butter" rentals or flips in subdivisions that I've owned multiple properties in and are very fairly similar to each other.

I have a buyer who works with me. I call him my "mini-me," because he goes out and does all the due diligence I used to do. He's been working with me for years, so for the most part, we're on the same page when it comes to analyzing deals.

I gotcha. When you know the area, that's a thought. I like to start with Google Maps. If I don't like what I see there, we're not going any further. Google Maps will give you an idea of what a neighborhood looks like, but the reality is, you better go see it unless you know it like the back of your hand.

Definitely. Something that you once said has stuck in my head: "Never fall in love with a deal. You fall in love with stealing a deal."

Talk about that a little bit, because I see investors fail to let the numbers make the decision, because they get emotional over a deal. I've always said that if the numbers don't make sense, the numbers don't make sense. The numbers are very simple to follow, but sometimes I see people who are eager to do a deal, or whatever force or urgency is driving them, and they'll fall in love with a deal despite the bottom line not being so glamorous. To me, that's all that really matters is that bottom line.

It all comes back to discipline. Discipline is a word that has to be written in big, black, bold letters in your mind—as big as you can see them. You never forget it, because you cannot be dying to do a deal. That is the kiss of death. When you do what we do, you're going to go through periods of time where you're going to come up dry for different reasons. For example, I come up dry as a private lender, because people are prepared to lend more than I lend.

When I go see a deal, if I like that deal — I may even love the deal, but I don't love it enough to go over my established criteria to lend more than my formula tells me to lend. No matter how much I love everything about the deal, I stop at a number and that's it. That's the discipline. So the only deal that you fall in love with is the deal that you end up doing that meets all of your criteria. Then you could say, "I'm in love." If it's not, you turn around like Mr. Wonderful from *Shark Tank* and you say, "That deal is now dead to me." There is a disciplined investor.

You watch him on *Shark Tank* and he tells you like it is. You don't like to hear it, but you should because this guy isn't doing it to insult you. He's just giving you the feedback from a disciplined investor's perspective. Now, could he be wrong? Yes, he's not perfect, but I'd put my money on him before I'd put my money on someone else who hasn't been there, done that, and proven they're successful.

There have been a few times that I can recall that you've given me and some of my students feedback that we didn't want to hear at first.

The very first year I was investing. I had done four or five deals up to that point and I had established a good relationship with my lender. But I got myself into a deal that was, at that time, way over my head in terms of the amount of rehab that it needed. The area was a little bit sketchy, and there were a few other issues. I met with my lender to talk about the deal, the rehab, and the other issues, and he kindly told me, "No, Brant, I can't loan to you on this one." I was stunned and a little pissed off as well.

I had somehow developed an ego after doing only four or five deals, and this guy had been in the business for at least 10 years and probably had loaned on hundreds of deals. But I found myself getting upset at this guy and asking myself, "Who is this guy to tell me no, that I can't do this?"

I decided to call other lenders to find someone else to fund the deal so I could prove to him that I was right. But then, during that process, I stopped said, "Wait a second, I've done four or five deals. This guy has probably done hundreds of deals. Maybe I should listen to what he has to say?"

I reevaluated and walked away from that deal. He was right, and I thanked him for it. Sometimes it's not the feedback we want to hear, but that's one of the we ways can learn from others without going through some of the pain we would have experienced had we not listened to them. This is also why having a coach or mentor can be so critical for people when they're just starting out.

Sometimes it's just that gut feeling inside that you get when looking at a deal, and that feeling is either positive or negative. I will tell you from experience, when we don't trust our gut feelings and we do the deal anyway, that's almost a guarantee that we are going to get smacked and we'll get hurt.

It's hard going for a while with no deals because you get hungry. Once you do deals and you know how to do deals, it's addictive. It's like your coffee in the morning. Can you go a whole day if you're addicted to coffee? How do you feel if you don't take your coffee in the morning? You feel like crap. So it's the same thing with deal making.

If you don't come across a deal within what you might consider a reasonable period of time, you start to get the jitters. That's where the word *discipline* comes back; that's what discipline is all about. It's not "Oh yeah, I'm disciplined, sure." Well, let's see you go three months without a deal and see how disciplined you are then? That's discipline.

You're right. Discipline is a powerful word. When we go through dry spells or have a low volume of deals, a lot of times that's a result of not having discipline in other areas.

For example, if you fail to have discipline in consistently marketing and networking for deals, the results speak for themselves. There are times we just go through buying slumps. It comes in waves. We'll go through a slow time, and then we'll go through times like now, where we have closed on 10 or 12 deals in the last 30 days. I know a lot of the little things that I do every day, phone calls, texts, meetings, meeting people, going to networking events, all of those disciplined efforts affect tomorrow and the next day and the next month and the next year.

You're planting your seeds. You must keep planting your seeds. I'd say discipline and patience work well together. You really have to learn how to calm yourself down and relax even though you're not relaxed. Even though you get up in the morning, you're ready to hit the ground running.

Running and athletics and business, it's all a head game. When you're able to relax your brain and go for a run, don't you get a better run if you're relaxed rather than if you're all uptight? I think it's discipline, patience, and being able to cool down even though you're dying to do your next deal. It's kind of like opening a safe. I use that as an example from time to time.

If a combination has three numbers and you only know two of the nubmers, you aren't opening that safe. So, you need to have the discipline; you need to have the patience. You need to have the formula and you need to have the drive. Make sure you have everything in your toolbox, and keep checking that toolbox, because sometimes you forget.

Sometimes we get lazy and complacent. I always look for ways to sharpen the sword, to stretch, and find ways to grow. I think we talked about this the other day, but right now I'm going through a program called

SealFit™. In less than two months from now, I'll be flying out to California to go through a two-day boot camp led by Navy Seals. I'll arrive on Friday morning at 8:00 a.m., and won't be done until sometime on Sunday afternoon. There will be no sleep whatsoever during that time. We'll be working out doing physical challenges in the hills, mountains, mud, and in the ocean around the clock for over 50 hours. Basically, it's the civilian version of the Navy Seal "Hell Week" that Navy Seals go through to become a Seal, but they actually go through a five-day crucible.

Physically, it's brutal. My family, friends, and clients ask me, "Why are you doing this? You're in your forties. You've had multiple knee and ankle surgeries. You've already done the Iron Man triathlons. Weren't those enough?"

You may remember I recently fought an MMA cage fight after only a few months' martial arts training.

The point is I'm going through SealFit™ because I know that the Navy Seals are some of the most disciplined men in the world and I know I can always improve my own discipline.

This training was created by Mark Divine, a former Navy Seal and a very successful businessman as well. I go through these physical experiences to strengthen my discipline. Some of my friends and family get it, and some of them don't, and that's fine with me.

This training really is not about the physical aspect that people see. It's actually about the mental side. One of Divine's main training platforms is called "Unbeatable Mind." He talks about how important this discipline is for all areas of our lives. And it is. The mental game affects my bottom line. It affects my business, how I parent my children, and how I lead my employees. It's so incredibly important. That's why I talk a lot about this as well. How we live our lives and how we live in our other areas of our lives affects our business.

That's one of the main reasons that I exercise and I train. It's not only that I want to look better and feel better, but it's really getting and keeping that mental toughness. The SealFit™ training experience I'm going through is called Kokoro, which essentially means a Warrior Spirit. Everyone who goes through the Kokoro event talks about the mental expansion after they leave. Sure, it's

physically tough—there's no doubt about it—
and there are standards we have to meet to
even get in and not get kicked out. There is a
high failure rate, but the ones that make it
all talk about the breakthroughs they get on
the mental side of things.

If you can master that mental game to
endure being physically brutalized for 50-
plus hours, when you come back to the real
world, everything is in slow motion. You're
moving at a faster pace than everybody else.

I'd like to talk a little more about fitness
and how this relates to business production.
I know that you had a period of time where
you were a bit overweight, and you made a
determination to change that.

I don't know if you know this, but I was
also about 50 pounds heavier than I am now
as well. I just got to a point where I kept
telling myself, "I don't feel good. I don't look
good. I'm just not happy in this state. I'm
just not happy like this." That's when I
started running.

Tell me about not only the importance of
taking care of yourself and how you run seven
miles a day now, but how that affects you
showing up to business meetings, looking at
deals, and just the energy that is there.

It comes back to discipline. I let myself go for I don't how many years, but if I had to take a guess, I would be ashamed to give you the number, because what happens—at least what happened to me, and I think most people might be able to relate to this—is that I basically put my business life ahead of me and everything else for a long period of time. So, the only thing that mattered was, how much money am I going to make tomorrow?

I would get up at 5:00 in the morning and go to bed at midnight, and do it seven days a week, and not take care of me. That worked for quite a long time. At least I thought it worked, until I guess it's probably three or four years ago now, when all of the illnesses that go along with being overweight began to come—and I was 80 pounds overweight. I am only 5' 7", so it was not a pretty sight. Over the years, I was developing all the illnesses that go along with being overweight.

You know me now, but you didn't know me then. If you see the two pictures beside each other, you'd say, "Oh, my God!" I started taking care of myself late in life. I have more respect for a guy like you than I have for a guy like me, because I should have been smart enough 30 years ago to take care of myself. You're smart enough to do it. My son who's 40, he's smart. He's also been smart enough to start it young and maintain it.

I got to the point where I was on more medication than I could count. It made me feel like crap. One day, I just said, "I know better than this. I'm going to turn this whole thing around, because this medication is killing me." I just woke up one morning and I said, "That's it, the party's over."

I started to eat right, because I knew how. I was just being lazy and undisciplined and not doing it. I started to exercise, and within six, nine months, maybe a year at the most, I was running five, six, seven miles per day and had dropped all the weight. The doctor took me off every medication except for one, which is a thyroid medication that apparently you never get off no matter what you do. That medication is a natural, not a chemical medication. So, it really has no effect on you.

Now, I feel a lot better. I'm as motivated as ever. That never changes, but I'm turning 66 this year. I look it, yes, I know. When I look in the mirror I say, "Oh crap, there's not much I could do about this," but I don't feel it, whereas if I would have kept that weight on, I probably would have felt 76 or 86.

I keep up with my 40-year-old son. When I'm with him, sometimes he's got to keep up with me, and that feels great. Before, I would have fallen behind. So I would say that it's helped me mentally as well and made me more disciplined.

You've heard the saying, "Do what you love and you'll never work a day in your life," but I know a lot of people that don't have that drive.

I went through a period of time of not only eating but also drinking a lot. I burned myself out while running my businesses, For a long period of time, I was getting up at 4:00 or 5:00 in the morning and working until midnight or later. I finally reached a point where I realized, "There's more to life than just money." I knew that I was neglecting the other areas of my life by chasing money and security. I made up my mind up years ago that I was going to figure out how to balance it all and pursue business, but not sacrifice relationships with my family, faith, or my own physical fitness. I also knew that my drive and the passion for real estate and business wasn't going to away, nor did I want it to.

The drive for business and making money is just inside of me. It's real, and I love this about myself and my life. I can't deny that I enjoy making money, but in my experience, when you begin to invest more into the other core areas of life, such as your faith, family/ loved ones, and health and fitness, you are so much more focused and energized in the business world and ultimately, you will make more money and have more fun.

People ask me all the time, "Where does that drive come from?" So, I want to ask you the same question and hear what would you say to people whom are either losing their drive or they just don't have it?

Everybody has a drive. They maybe haven't figured it out, haven't faced it, or haven't changed their life around to do what they want to do. I have a friend who is in his early seventies now. He worked in the oil and gas business as a drafter all his life.

He worked all his life and a couple of years ago, when the bust hit and they let him go. Suddenly, he didn't know what to do. You know what he does every day? He does what he loves now. He's into cars. He works on cars for himself. This guy loves the old cars. So, he goes to the car shows, and he bought himself a couple of old cars, and he's tinkering with them and changing parts and doing all this.

So, was he happy working for somebody else? No, but I guess he just wasn't able to do what he really wanted to do, because he couldn't figure out how to make a living out of it, but I think that something motivates every person. It may not be what we like, and if it's not what we like but a person doesn't like what we like, and they're doing it just because it's fashionable at the time, they're making the wrong decisions.

It's not going to work. So everybody, if they look deep down inside, has something that excites them, and everyone has something that motivates them. I think a lot of people suffer from that problem, and they go their whole lives doing stuff they really never wanted to do. I wasn't born in the real estate business. I didn't have a clue that I was going to do this one day. If you think back to your childhood, did you ever think you were going to be doing what you're doing today? No way.

So, how did you decide that this was something that motivated you? Do you even remember that?

 I do. I was at that point in life where I was burned out in the corporate world. We went to visit my wife's family on the East Coast for a reunion. My wife had told me about a distant family member who was very wealthy. I knew that he was an entrepreneur and that was about it. So I tried to get to know him, pick his brain a little bit. Although it was a short conversation, he talked to me about real estate, and the few words he spoke changed my trajectory completely.

He talked about how he started out buying houses, then small apartment buildings, and really he encouraged me to take action and do some deals. It was just a seed, a little bitty seed that he gave me. I said to myself, "Okay, I can read a book." So, I began reading books and went to networking clubs and that was it. I think there is something called the Michael Jordan Rule, or the 10,000-Hour Rule. It may have been in one of Malcolm Gladwell's books.

Anyway, it says that to really become great at something, you really need to spend about 10,000 hours doing it. So I began with my first hour by reading a book and I've been adding on hours ever since.

You have to love it or you'll never make it to the 10,000 hours. You're right, I tell this to a lot of people. I had a conversation with someone yesterday who's just starting out, and he said, "I need to get my business cards and an LLC set up and this and that." I told him, "Look, the fact is you haven't done a deal yet. How about you do some deals first to make sure this is something you're going to enjoy and be committed to?"

This business isn't for everyone, so I want them to make sure that this is something that they really want to do, and if it is, great. The difference, I think, for me is whenever there is a challenging time in the market or a setback, I think, "What do I need to do to get through this to find the next opportunity in this situation?"

A lot of people would give up and close up shop and that's okay if they weren't committed or passionate about this business. I plan on doing this till the day I die. It's just in my DNA...

We need to realize that we need to reinvent ourselves from time to time. That's part of the fun and part of the challenge. If we don't have a challenge, we aren't having fun. Things change, and people have to go with the flow. As I said earlier, you have to keep your antennae up and continue to be sensitive to what's happening around you. Then you can be proactive and start changing your targets.

When I was a kid, there were different targets out there in the world than there are today. Things change, but real estate isn't going to change. You're always going to have—at least in our lifetime—brick and mortar. A lot of the things that we have now in real estate are going to stay constant, but the economic environment changes. When that changes, then we just change with it.

It's not difficult, and it's not frightening. It's actually fun, because the fundamentals remain the same. Whether you're buying a house, fixing it and flipping it, or you're building a house from the ground up or spec to sell, you're buying an office building, a hotel, a strip center, or a parking garage, whatever it may be, the fundamentals really don't change; the economic situation changes.

For example, three or four years ago, I wasn't doing any business in the single-family-home arena. I had office buildings, hotels, parking garages, apartments, stuff like that. But then the world changed. The world changed, at least in this city, to the point where the office buildings, the office market, the hotels, all that different stuff was going to become overbuilt.

Everyone else was focusing on building more apartments here. As you know, I usually go the other way. I try to be a bit of a contrarian. When I start to see too much excitement in one asset type, I say, "No, there's too much going on." I remember, as a kid, playing musical chairs. When the music stopped, if you didn't have a seat, you were out. When there are too many people chasing seats, we all know the music stops.

Watch them, because they are going to go the wrong way. I just said, "Okay, no office buildings, no hotels, none of this, none of that, but the single-family...." There was a pent-up demand; there was a need. Although people were in it, there was some more need.

So I just said, "Okay." There's no magic to doing a home instead of an office building. The exit strategy may be different. That's okay, there may not be recurring income if you're going to build it and sell it, but we can assess it the same way: location, location, location. Either it's a great location or it isn't.

You're not going to change that. If it's a crappy location, you don't touch it. So I dove into it. That's what reinventing yourself is all about. When I looked around one day, I said, "No." I'm getting killed if I go out and I build apartments now, or if I build office buildings in this city now, then I'm going to get killed. So I just stopped. It's not what I do. I invest; that's what I do. I invest in real estate. I don't invest in businesses, because I don't understand them. I reinvented myself and then built it up slowly, kept that discipline, figured out a formula. It's almost four years later and I've never had to foreclose on one borrower since I began private lending. That's why reinventing yourself is important.

Let's talk more about you as a private lender rather than as an investor.

When a borrower comes to you, what are you looking for from the borrower? What are the principles or fundamental things you're looking for from them, or not looking for?

I can spend 20 or 30 minutes with a borrower, probably, at the most, and maybe quicker than that typically. One of the important things for me is to make sure they know what they're doing. So, if a borrower hasn't done this before and they're coming to me, it's their first time and they've never done what they're planning to do, that concerns me. Everybody deserves a first chance, and when I started, I had never done it before. I get it, but as a lender, I'm looking at it differently.

If I like the borrower, if I like what they're doing, if I think they've got the smarts but have never done it before, I will suggest that I introduce them to someone I know that's been there, done that—that's bought it, fixed it up, and sold it or that's built it and sold it.

If they're willing to meet someone like that, like yourself, or take on a mentor that I trust, then great.

You're a perfect example. If a new investor comes along and they haven't done it before, but I know you are behind them as their coach or partner—you've run the budget; you've looked at the property; your contractors are going to do all the work—then I know it's going to get done and it's getting done right, because one of biggest risks for a lender is whether the house is going to be finished and is the work going to be the right quality? Is it going to pass inspection when the new owner wants to get a mortgage to buy it?

I'm not in the lending business to take properties back, and I think that most lenders are probably not either. There are some predatory lenders, but basically, we just want the yield. We want to sleep at night, and we don't want to have to build that house and finish it. So that's a key component.

I also like to see skin in the game. There are different schools of thought on that, and I kind of go along with both schools, whereas if you bought it so cheap, why do I need to put skin in the game? I look at that and I think about it. I haven't seen anybody buy so cheap that I feel comfortable lending them 100 percent or almost 100 percent, but my underwriting is a lot more conservative than most. I see a lot of people getting loans that I wouldn't do, because the underwriting from the lender is much more aggressive, and I get it. I understand it and say, "Hey, that's great." I'm not insulted. I'm actually grateful for the opportunity and say, "Thank you for calling me and allowing me to bid on the deal." But the other thought for me also is that when someone has skin in the game, they have an interest. They're less likely to walk away, and I don't want them to walk away.

If you've got skin in the game, you want to save it, whereas if you have no skin in the game and things get difficult, some people will walk and some people won't. I know you wouldn't, because we've had that discussion, but you never know who might. Even the strongest borrower with the most experience can get into a bad situation to where they do something they would never think they would have to do. I want skin in the game for that reason.

We've bought properties from private lenders that they had to take back from borrowers because times got tough and the borrowers walked. I got one deal from a hard money lender because the borrower walked. The borrower they foreclosed on was very well to do financially. He had skin in the game, but not a lot. The hard money company trusted him because of his business background, but when things got tough, you know the rest of the story, he bailed on the deal of course.

You simply don't know how people are going to react to situations. If they don't have skin in the game, then it's easier for them to walk away, but like I mentioned, they can walk with skin in the game as well, but at least your position is well covered if it comes to that.

I know that when I first partnered with people and borrowed private money, it was very humbling to me. My wife and I lived in an apartment. We didn't have any money. We had just finished paying off student loans and credit cards, and had our first child. We were broke and living paycheck to paycheck. Then one day I told my wife, "I'm going to become a real estate investor," and she said, "Are you nuts? How are you going to do that?" I said, "I don't really know. I haven't figured that out just yet."

Fast-forward a couple of years later and 20-plus deals later, we had moved into a house, and I began working with private lenders. I told my wife about the private lenders that were investing with me. I explained to her, "People are beginning to loan money to me from their IRAs and some with their cash. This is their retirement and their wealth. This is what they've worked their whole lives for. They're investing it with me so I can do more deals." She said, "That's great," and I responded, "It is great. However, I'm still pretty new at this. I've been doing this two years, and if anything goes bad or sideways, I need your backing on this, because I'm letting you know that my investors get paid first, and we'll sell everything we have, including our own home, to pay them back first. We'll live out on the streets if we have to because my investors are getting paid." That's been my attitude. I've never told a lender that, but I think that they feel it or sense it, because that's what I'm committed to, and my lenders have been incredibly loyal to me over the years.

I typically borrow 100% of the purchase price and repairs, so for most of my deals, I don't have skin in the game. My skin is what I'm determined to do, and that is that I'm going to make that deal work no matter what, and that mindset is really critical. I think a good track record counts for something as well. I've done close to 200 deals now and I've never not performed on a loan. I also personally guarantee all my deals, so I cover my lenders from that perspective.

How do you feel about an investor that comes in and they don't have any money? I feel for these guys, because I understand where they're coming from, because that's also how I got started. You mentioned maybe partnering with someone. How do you feel about if they get a second lien to make the deal work? What are your thoughts on that?

When I have a borrower that has no money of their own to use, that doesn't bother me. I get it; we're not born with money. We have to make it, and we have to make it on a few deals. So, I suggest that they find some friends and family that might want to invest with them. I have no problem if they put a second lien after me. As a matter of fact, I love it, because there's someone there that's going to try to save their investment. It's a great thing.

Just recently, I brought a friend of mine into a deal that was a hard money deal that went bad (not mine). The second lienholder, who put up the money for the borrower, had to foreclose on the borrower, because the borrower did not perform.

So that person took over the ownership of the project, called in someone like yourself who they knew, and that person knew what they were doing, but this particular person didn't have the money that I required for them to put in. So, I brought a friend to the table, and he's putting in $100,000 and partnering up with the general contractor, and we're getting the deal done that way. He's getting a second lien, and I'll have the first lien. I'll put in $250k, and he'll put in $100k, and he'll be their partner.

I've never done that before. My friend trusts me, and that bothers me a bit, because I'm not guaranteeing him his money. He's my buddy and I don't want him to lose any money. So, I'm getting him extra protection on his investment that other people wouldn't normally get from the borrowers. I try to help people make deals that I like, as long as my exposure is not greater than my comfort level. I like a lot of margin.

Recently, more people than ever have been reaching out to us that are considering becoming private lenders and wanting to invest in our deals. Many baby boomers are retiring now, and they don't trust the stock market. People are much more aware about self-directed IRAs as well as how advantageous they are to invest in real estate with. What are some of the big tips that you would give someone who's thinking about being a private lender?

Folks looking to get into the private lending arena need to be extremely cautious. Real estate is fashionable today. It's in vogue now, and that's all people probably talk about when they're at parties, over lunch especially, because all these folks that have money. There's a lot more of them today, and there's going to be a lot more coming up through the ranks, because these people are having a difficult time achieving any type of yield on their money. I had the same problem, and it's a first-class problem to have.

There's nothing to be ashamed of with having that problem, but when I said to you earlier that I've been doing it for almost four years and I've had no foreclosures, that means I haven't lost a dime. I've loaned millions, probably tens of millions, because the loans pay off and you're on a treadmill, which is fine. I love the treadmill, but you've got to remember where I'm coming from. I was like you. I borrowed from hard money lenders when I got started in real estate.

When I first began, I was the borrower and I borrowed big money, because I did big deals. I borrowed millions on each deal, but that's how I got my education. Not only was I the borrower, the investor, the developer or the rehabber, but I was also paying attention to the guys I borrowed from. These guys were, not knowingly—and me not knowingly at the time—preparing me for when my time came.

I'm going to be 66 this year. Twenty-five years ago, I was borrowing from hard money lenders that today have either passed away or they're 85, 90 years old. They were shrewd, but so was I, because my shrewdness was in choosing the right deal. I knew my money was expensive, but I was okay with that, because I bought the deal right so that the cost of my money meant nothing to me.

They taught me by lending to me. When I started three, four years ago, I was familiar with both sides and I was disciplined. I wasn't hungry to the point I was desperate. Everything sounds wonderful at the cocktail parties. You're probably not going to hear too many horror stories at the cocktail party, at least not yet.

But it's coming. The market has become frothier, as you know. You're an investor. You told me earlier the deal you paid $100k for ten years ago, you're paying $150k in today's market. As we all know, nothing goes up forever. Whatever goes up must come down. We call it gravity, and really, it's supply and demand, because you get to a certain point, right? So I'm not sitting here and telling you that you can't make money being a private lender.

You're not sitting here and telling me, "Hey, I'm paying $150k instead of $100k," that you can't do deals and make money. That's not what either one of us has really said. What I'm saying is, you have to become more cautious as the market gets frothier, and you really need to know what you're doing.

If you don't know what you're doing, then it's likely you're getting killed. You're getting your head handed to you, and you know that and I know that, because it's happening now. You told me stories and I also told you stories earlier about a few different situations. I think it was off the record. Maybe we were just chatting about how and where things are changing. So, if these folks can find someone who's got the experience and just wants to help others not make mistakes, they need to get around the table with someone who's not motivated to lend their money out for them. There are folks out there that make money by lending out other people's money. They are not taking care of business. They are motivated to put the money out, that's it.

They're not conservative enough, and they're going to get hurt and hurt others. I learned a long time ago not to invest in a business I don't understand. Earlier you mentioned he 10,000-hour rule to figure out how to do it right. Don't be ashamed of not knowing how to invest your money, because if you invest it without knowing, I promise you're losing. I can tell you a lot of stories about that.

I don't invest in businesses because I don't understand them. I don't know that formula. I suppose I could try to figure it out, but I'm so collateral minded that I would apply the same principles to lending to a business, and I'd look for the real estate in the business. I'd look for the tangible assets, but it doesn't have to be only real estate. I've taken other assets as additional collateral from borrowers to give me the comfort I need to lend them the money they need to do their deal. I certainly wouldn't lend on a piece of equipment if I had no idea what the heck it was going to be worth 10 days from now. It would have to be a real asset.

These people need to be educated, and they don't need to be educated by the people that want to lend out their money for them— not borrow, lend.

 The book of Proverbs talks about how a fool and his money are soon parted. I think it's really important, because I help some family

members invest their money with other investors. It's self-directed IRA funds, so I don't borrow from them. I help them direct their IRA to other investors, and, knock on wood, we have a perfect track record so far.

I will say that I haven't loaned out nearly as much as you have, but I educate them first and foremost. Really, it comes down to understanding what you're investing in.

I will probably always invest in real estate myself. I've begun to personally loan money on other investors' deals and more people are beginning to reach out to me to loan to them. It will, as far as I can tell, always be real estate that I loan on as well, because that's what I know and what I understand and that's how I'll sleep best at night.

You've probably heard the saying, "Don't put all of your eggs in one basket," but I've also heard it said, "Put all your eggs in one basket, and make sure no one tips over your basket." I'm going to do everything I can to protect my basket, and I believe strongly in this philosophy. This real estate basket is what I know, and this is my expertise and this is where all of my eggs are. That's what I tell people that are interested in becoming a private lender, and unfortunately, I get calls from lenders who've already done a bad deal, and that's never a fun call to take.

These calls typically go something like, "I loaned to a guy that I thought knew what he was doing," and you know the rest of the story. Maybe the person they loaned to did know what he was doing, to a certain extent, but when he hit some opposition on the deal, he bailed for whatever reason. A lot of times, new private lenders are drawn to the idea of earning 12-14 percent or other high rates that newbie real estate investors will pay.

I understand it. High rates of return of very appealing to them. They call me to comparison shop, and I tell them, "Well, we usually pay somewhere between 6% to 9%, and occasionally 10%, depending on the deal." They look at a 7% return, for example, versus 12%, and it seems like a no-brainer to take the 12%. But what they may or may not understand, unfortunately, is the experience factor. I've heard it said, "You can tell the experience of the investor by what he pays for his money." A lot of times, the real estate investors that these newbie private lenders are working with who are going to pay 12-15 percent are likely to be inexperienced, and with that lack of experience is an increased possibility the lender may have to foreclose and take that deal back.

Yes, they have financial issues, because there have been times where we're tapped out as well, and the numbers on the deal are phenomenal. Even if we're paying 12 percent, it still makes sense. So, I'm more than glad to pay 12, 15... I'll pay 50 percent interest if the numbers make sense.

I don't have a problem with that, providing everything else fits with the deal. Like I explained to you before – I'm putting in $250k and someone's putting $100k in. This person has been there, done that, and he knows how to build them. Everything fits, but from an inexperienced-lender viewpoint, you're not going to be able to come to the table and tell me that, "Yeah, I'm making 14% plus three points on this deal." As an inexperienced lender, you're going to go, "Wow, man, that's what I need," but at the same time, you're not going to be able to sit there and tell me that if there's a problem, you can get that house finished.

I can. I'll make a couple of phone calls and the house is done. I'm foreclosed. Whatever state it's in, I'm not afraid. I have borrowers that would love to come in, take a piece of the deal, finish the house, put it up for sale, and I keep my hands clean.

I've had borrowers come to me and say, "Look, lend me X amount of dollars. I need another 50 grand for the rehab. I'll put it in as I finish the deal," and I say, "Sure you will, but I'll hold your $50k, and I'll release it to you as you progress so that I know you've got the money, I know that it's getting finished, and we're going to get lien waivers. We're going to take care of business." When the person tells me, "No, I don't think so," I say, "Well then, no, I don't think so either," but I've been there, done that

I don't know everything. Nobody knows everything. My concern for the inexperienced investor is just that. They don't know enough to analyze the deal properly upfront, or if the deal gets into trouble, they don't know how to pull themselves out. As good as my underwriting may be, a day is going to come when I'm going to have a problem. Although, I may be in at the right number, if I don't know whom to call to come in and finish the project, I'm not going to be able to sell it.

That's something big. I call it "Staying Power." I've heard it also referred to as "Handling the Downside," and I also relate this around the conversation of always having multiple exit strategies when it comes to real estate deals.

For example, in my real estate business with single-family homes, I've done low-end hood houses, and I've done super high-end, close to a million-dollar homes, and of course, I've done about 80 percent of my deals with houses that are right in the middle price point for our market. Our sweet spot is right in the middle. I love it for many reasons, but the main reason is because we have the most staying power in that medium-priced-home range.

Yes, if the market goes up, we may lose some buyers and renters, but at the same time, we've got buyers and renters coming up. Vice versa, when the market goes down, we will lose some buyers and renters, but we've got buyers and renters coming down from the higher-end market at the same exact time. So, when we're playing with houses in the middle, we can typically sell those houses in any market, or we can rent them out and have cash flow.

We have other options available as well, such as owner financing, which I love, or we can dump it and sell it to an investor. We have staying power and can handle the market fluctuations.

What would you say are a couple of things that someone, as a private lender, can look at to give themselves the ability to handle that downside, if or when it comes? If you do this enough, it's a matter of when, not if.

It's going to happen. I guess, as a lender, how I look at it is, I'm using my money. I'm not borrowing money to invest in the loan. A lot of people take their loans and go to the bank and pledge them as collateral and borrow 50, 60, 70, 80 percent of that loan amount, as much as the bank will lend them, because money is cheap today, and they're leveraging their deals. Now, I could do that too.

I had lunch with a banker this week who sends me business and would love to lend me money against my loans. I haven't done that, because I know that the day will come when there will be problems. If I haven't leveraged my loans and I foreclose, then I have enough money to pay insurance, pay taxes, pay utilities, etc. Even though you have no leverage, you have costs. The name of the game in real estate is, "just wait." The longer you wait, the more money you make. As long as you can afford to wait, then you will make more money than you would have made by just lending on it, because that's just how it goes.

If you're not leveraging, and you have enough cash reserves, you can't get greedy. Greed will kill you. If you lend out the last penny you've got just because you're so greedy you want every last dime working for you, and then you have a problem, and you need cash reserves to get through a slow time, and you don't have them, you've got a problem.

My dad always said to me, "The bank gives you an umbrella on a sunny day, but when it rains, they take it back." So, whenever times get tough, there's never any money out there, and you need to remember that.

If you need it, there's no loan. Although you can make more money if you leverage your loan, my attitude has been not to do that. The biggest problem I've had is lending out all my money, because I'm very picky on the deals. I haven't been in a position where I've got a deal and I don't have the money, but I thought about that. What do I do if I've got more deals than I have money? What do I do?

I have two choices. I can either go to the bank, or I can find someone to participate in the loans with me where we're all cash in the deal and we don't have a problem. I wouldn't make as much money as if I borrowed from the bank, because I'll pay the bank about four or five percent and then loan out at 15 percent and make ten percent on the spread. If someone participates with me, I may only make 3 or 4 percent, but I have no downside.

Nobody's knocking on my door, saying, "Hey, your borrower is in default. You need to pay me off this loan, because your loan has no more value to me." That's what the bank is. The bank says, "I'll lend you money against your loans, absolutely, love to do it, but as soon as one of your borrowers goes in default and stops making their payments to you, you need to pay me off on that loan." They're gone, and I want out. So, again, it's the old umbrella story. Now, I'll lend to you as long as things are going well. As soon as things aren't going well, guess what, I want my money back.

I've got people that want to participate with me as lenders. I just can't...I'm having trouble finding enough deals to lend out my money. That's the good news and the bad news. There's a group in California that told a friend who is in the business with me, "You've got $25 million. We'll participate with you," he says. My response, "Thank you, but I can't lend it out." Now, if we did what all the other sharks are doing, we could, but we won't. We'll forego that. We won't make all that money, because we don't want to take the risk. Even though it's other people's money, and we would have money in every deal too, I just don't want to deal with that.

It's the tortoise and the hare, and usually the turtle is going to win the race. Lenders will come to us and say, "I heard this guy, and he'll pay 12 percent, and you're only going to pay seven percent." And I'll say, "I understand that, and if you can make 12 percent and you don't have to take the deal back, and you're able to put that money to work over the long-term, I would take the 12 percent deal if I were you."

However, if you can invest that same money at seven to nine percent on a safer deal with a more established investor, and that money is going to stay in the market, invested and earning you a return, and it's not sitting on the sidelines, meaning you're not having to constantly recycle that money, you're going to earn a very nice return. Some people have $100,000 to invest, or maybe $200,000 or $300,000, or even as little as $25,000, it really doesn't matter. If you look at eight or nine percent rate of return that's constantly working versus 12 percent that is only invested for six to nine months out of the year and then it's parked again and not working for three or four months, the tortoise is going to win the race over the long-term. Then, if a lender has to take back a deal that goes sideways and you weren't properly protected... uh-oh, no you're in trouble.

There's just not enough juice for them. I know the way that you run your private lending business, you're going to come out ahead because you know how to manage the asset if things go sideways, you're just going to have to do work that you don't want to do, which for you is really making a few phone calls. But I love your insight on this for new private lenders and I agree 110%, they have to be educated and they have to safeguard their position. They really need to verify the borrower is experienced or working with someone who's experienced, and that they have some skin in the game.

Yes, then we all come out ahead, but I think that's incredible insight and wisdom for people that are looking at you. You have to be educated. You have to safeguard your position. You have to verify the borrower is experienced or working with someone who's experienced, and that they have some skin in the game.

Basically, as a private lender, they must take matters into their own hands. But for those who play this game the right way, that's the beautiful thing about real estate – there is an opportunity and it's here and now. We're talking about crowd funding and group funding for deals and it's a really good thing when people do it the right way, but it can be really, really ugly if they do it the wrong way.

They must take matters into their own hands. That's the beautiful thing about real estate – there is an opportunity and it's here now. We're talking about crowd funding and group funding. It's a really good thing when people do it the right way, but it can be really, really ugly if they do it the wrong way.

James, I really appreciate you taking the time to share your wisdom. I know you've been a great asset and mentor to me and to others. I appreciate everything that you've shared with me over the last couple of years since we've known each other.

It's been a lot of fun for me. I'm glad to be able to help people not fall into the wrong trap and to help them be able to get things done right.

When it comes to coaching and teaching people, I say, "I love to motivate, educate, inspire, and to equip people to take action through in their lives and their businesses and create the results they desire."

I definitely feel you helped me carry out my mission with my followers and with the readers of this book. So, I can't say thank you enough.

It was my pleasure. Good luck to everybody.

PART II –
THE MASTERMIND

I was honored to have James come speak to the Men during a session at one of my "Breakthrough at the Beach" events.

Breakthrough at the Beach is a personal development, business, and real estate mastermind where my trainers and I take a small group of men through a three-day boot camp experience to help them to launch and grow their real estate investing businesses while also providing personal development training in spirituality, family relationships and health/ fitness training.

I'm proud to share the many insights that James shared that day with those men here with you in this book. Enjoy.

Guys, this is James, whom I told you all about. He's one of my mentors, in addition to many other things. He's a private lender, a successful businessman, a real estate investor, and an entrepreneur. He has a wealth of knowledge in regard to not only real estate, but life in general, and I'm honored to have him here today.

Thanks for having me. It is my pleasure to be here. I'm happy to share my experience and knowledge to hopefully help you guys develop your real estate career, or any other business you choose to do. By coming here today, I learned something that I didn't know from a previous discussion I had with Brant. That's why I love participating and networking with people. No matter how long you've been doing this, someone's going to teach you something. What I learned today is very valuable, so thank you again, Brant. In my lending business, I need to keep that in the back of my mind, to always keep an ear to the street to learn about things that are changing.

I guess what I'm going to try to do is give you all a little bit of my life history. I hope you don't fall asleep while I am doing it. I'll try to keep it exciting and interesting. I'll give you some reference points so you can kind of connect the dots.

I turned 65 last November and I run seven miles per day. I do that to stay healthy and so I don't have to take any medications other than one pill a day. I find that it keeps my mind clear; it reduces my stress, because even though I am successful today, we all have stresses that are just natural to us in our daily lives. I know the biggest thing for me is I just can't stop working. When I get up in the morning, I face the day as though I had to make money that day like I did 50 years ago. I don't have to, but I do it anyway, because I enjoy it. I guess because I've been on this treadmill for so long, it's just in my veins. It doesn't stop, and that's good news and bad news. I consider it good because if I didn't have something to do, I'd be in real trouble.

I'll give you a little history on me as an individual. I had a burning desire before I hit my teens to get out and go to work and make something of myself. As an example, in my youth, when all my friends were on Christmas vacation—we were 12 years old—I didn't go on vacation; I found a job. I worked during the Christmas holidays to make money. That's the kind of drive I have. I've always tried to think of what really made me drive that way. I'm not really quite sure. I keep relating to what I saw in my home. My dad was a mechanic, and he came home every day with grease on his hands. That really bothered the crap out of me. I didn't want to be in that position. His income was limited and things were tight. I used to hear my parents talking about the finances, and there was never enough money. I think that was a big driving force for me, which is good news. It was bad news at the time but, ultimately, helped me create really good news in my life.

I really wanted to work. When I turned 17, I dropped out of high school. My parents were livid, and they did everything in their power to try to convince me to stay in school, but I just didn't want to. I wanted to go to work.

Looking back, I regret it in one aspect. If I had gone through the formal education and accomplished what my wife and I forced our son to do because we saw the errors of my ways, I believe I would have been more successful and more well-rounded. I would have been better able to read contracts. I still would rely on an attorney though. My son went to law school, but he doesn't practice. He is an entrepreneur as well, but I can see the difference between how he looks at a contract or a business versus how I do.

So, at 17 years old, I went to work with a burning desire. I did anything they asked me to do because I wanted to climb the ladder. One of the first jobs I had was cleaning toilets, and I didn't mind it! I didn't mind, because I wanted to show them I could clean a toilet faster and better than anybody else and then let me move to the next level. And they did.

So, at the next company I went to work for, I started off cleaning toilets, and then I ended up being in sales soon after. I was successful in sales within a year or two. Then, I got offers from other people to come work for them, until eventually, I went out on my own as a salesperson, and I worked on commission only. They wanted to offer me draws, but I refused the draws, because with draws came a lower commission rate. If you don't take any draws, then you get the highest commission you can get. That's what I wanted.

I had no money, and I was starving. Yeah, zero. I struggled to put gas in my Beetle—my car, that's what they called the Volkswagen in those days. So, I put together a little sales agency. I found some great products in the ladies' garment business. I was twentyish, then and I was making more money than I could spend. And that, of course, wasn't enough, I wanted to make more.

I started to meet people that were very wealthy, and you need to understand that I knew nothing. There was no business in the house. My father didn't have the business acumen to share with me that I was able to share with my son. When I came out of my parents' house, I was as green as could be. When my son came out of the house, he was ready to do deals, and he did. He made his first million dollars in real estate in his first year of law school. What a difference!

It's amazing how you can help your children if you have the right tools to help them. My parents didn't have the tools. They were good people and they kept me on the straight and narrow, but they couldn't give me what they didn't know. So, I learned that from the streets.

I was successful at making money in the garment industry. I met successful people that were seasoned, and I would ask them,

"What's next? How do I get really rich?" They all kept saying real estate, real estate. And I would think to myself, "Okay, real estate?" So, I would leave the room and say to myself, "Okay, real estate, what am I supposed to do now? What are they talking about with real estate?"

So, I decided to educate myself, because in those days—and I'm going back, well, I'm 65 now, so I'm going back 45 years—cell phones and the Internet didn't exist yet! There were books for sale in bookstores, because again, no Internet. I bought every book on the shelf about how to make money and those types of things. Took them out. Bought them. Read them from cover to cover, and went, "Okay, I get it."

So, I went looking for a product. There was no Internet so we would search through the newspapers to find a product. I read ads every day, and called brokers looking for a product. By then, I was married and I had already saved a couple hundred thousand dollars. It was a significant amount of money then, and it's a lot of money now if you don't have any. It was a nice little nest egg to start with. So, I decided, I'm going to go into multi-family.

My first multi-family deal was 16 units. I paid a hundred grand for the property. It was a distressed property that the owner inherited it from his dad. He was an older guy, and he didn't have a clue. So, any time when it came up for lease renewal, the residents would complain about the rents and he would lower them! So, I thought, "Okay, this is perfect for me." I bought it for $100,000 or $150,000 and I assumed the mortgage at the time. By the way, I'm a Canadian, and this was in Montreal.

I put down $50,000 out of pocket. I know, I read all the books, where it says you could do it with no money down, but I had money. I figured, I'll put it to work.

So, I put down $50,000 and I dove in. We cleaned it up, renovated it, fixed it up, raised the rent, of course, and within nine months, I sold it and I doubled my money! I thought, "This is a good business." I couldn't do that in what I was doing before. I had to work, really work hard. There's a difference working in real estate. I don't feel like I'm working when I'm doing real estate, but in my job, I really had to hustle selling garments. Real Estate is ridiculously easy compared to the garment industry. In that business, you had this very short life, meaning a short shelf life in that business, because once you went into your thirties and forties, they blew you off and looked to the younger guys. This was just the way it worked. So, my goal was really to build something and then move into that business.

So, I went from owning 16 units, to a 32-unit deal, and I did the same thing, and then I went to 325 units in one deal. Here's how I got there even though I didn't have enough money to do the 325-unit deal from first glance. I was doing extremely well in my sales business, and I had made relationships with a lot of people that would come to me because I had the rights to sell a very desirable product. I was the man you had to get to, which was impressive, and I parlayed that with these guys, because they were all business people buying products. I told them about my little real estate deals, and when it came to the big one, everybody had an interest and wanted to participate. In those days, there were no hard money lenders. It didn't exist. So, it was friends and family, which you can still do today.

I had a couple of guys that I knew very well that did what I had done. I made deals with them, and I would take multiple liens on deals. I'm talking second, third, fourth, and fifth liens on my deals, whatever it took to get the deal done. I must have gone up to ten. It was awesome. I was giving them an interest rate only—no participation or equity.

Then what happened? It went up in value a lot. The property was a mess. It was so mismanaged, but it was great. That's what I wanted. I got in there, rolled up my sleeves, and left my other job. Well, my company just stopped, and I closed it up. I managed this full-time and handled it myself. I became the manager and did whatever it took to make this property successful.

This was where I learned how to become a real estate investor and found that it really comes down to applying some basic business principles: finding out what people want, what the competition is not doing, what I can do to make myself better than the competition, and how to outperform the competition. And that's what I did.

When I bought it, the property was maybe 80 percent occupied. Nobody wanted to live there. Rents were low. The property looked like crap. I fixed it up and then had a waiting list within six months, and the rents were just skyrocketing. Within a year, I sold that property and walked away with a check for over two million dollars.

I kept a copy of that check, but I don't know what I did with it. That was my first home run, you know. From there, I just kept going. I never let success get to my head—never! To me, I think of myself the same as I was 45 years ago.

Remember that one bad mistake can suck up a bunch of money. Stay firm in your chair and use the same principles. You have more experience now, so you may be able to avoid some pitfalls.

I did another big deal after that, another apartment, okay—two high-rises. Same kind of deal, and we made a home run there too. After that deal, I ended up negotiating with a broker that came to my office one day and had some property to show me, and he really had nothing that I really felt I wanted to sink my teeth into. As he was leaving my office, I said, "That's all you got?" He said, "Well, I got a big one, but this is too big for you." I said, "Get your ass back here." He put this thing on the table, and it's a big one. It's a hotel with 500 rooms in it and an office building with half a million square feet, all at one complex. 200,000 sq. ft. of underground retail space and two 2,000-car underground parking garages - all financially underwater.

It's in trouble, mismanaged. So, this deal is right down my alley and exactly what I'm looking for, and he said, "You don't have the money to do this deal, so don't worry about it." I said, "I'm making an offer." So, I made an offer. I took a shot.

A couple of weeks go by, and the asset manager who's representing the lender that took it back calls me and says, "I'd like to meet with you." I said, "Oh, my pleasure." So, I think at that time, I'm a kid and I'm still in my twenties or early thirties. I was young; I really was wet behind the ears.

I put on a coat and tie, which is not my style as you can see, but I figured I better dress nice. I went to his office and we talked, and he said, "You know, I like you." I said, "Okay, I like you too." He said, "I'm going to let you put this deal under contract and tie it up." So, I said, "Great, how much earnest money do you want?" He said, "Give me a check for a hundred thousand, but I'm not going to cash it. I am going to keep it at my desk." I said, "My pleasure."

So, I tie up this huge complex. I really have no money in the deal, and it's way too big for me, but I think that I know a lot of people; let me see what I could do.

The first weekend I had control of the project, I sold the hotel at a cocktail party. Can you believe that? I knew that I had to take the hotel out of the whole transaction, because hotels are a lot different than office buildings and retail and parking. It's just a different animal. A person that would buy the office building and the retail would be afraid to touch the hotel, unless they were someone like me, because I'd do that too. But at that time, I figured this was the safest thing to do.

So, I flipped it, and then I was left with the rest. Before you know it, I started getting calls from the biggest guys in town, wanting to buy the paper from me. Perfect! I had three or four bidders, and I ended up selling the paper to the guys behind the scenes who were the owners of a distillery company.

I never met them. I just worked with their people during the process. I also met a senator who was involved somehow on this deal. Then I met a guy named Peter, and I developed a great relationship with him. I sold him the deal, and I sold him the paper. He paid me a couple of million bucks for it, and I made them put the cash up first. I don't care who you are, you've got to show me the money, and they showed me the money. They put it in my trust account. You get it, you got the deal.

Peter was a worldly guy, and I was just a young, hungry guy. I said, "Peter, I've got a real problem." He asked, "What's that?" I replied, "I don't know where to go from here. The market here in Montreal is at its peak.". There were no deals there. At least no deals with upside left. The pricing was so high that I could buy, but I couldn't buy anything depressed like I liked them. All I needed to do was get it up to the price I was paying for it. So, that's not for me.

He said, "I think I know what you need to do. You need to go to the oil patch." This was around 1986 to 1987. I said, "The oil patch, what the hell is that?" Well, that's Calgary, Edmonton, Houston, and Dallas. I said, "Why would I want to go to those places?" He said, "Because they are busts, and you want an opportunity, that's where you've got to go."

So, I got on a plane, and I eventually chose Houston for a variety of reasons. I think the biggest reason was it was in the US, which I thought was a better place for me to be than Canada. Canada is a lot more restrictive and not as invested in real estate and as friendly as the US, tax wise and mentality wise. And it looked to me like Houston had taken the hardest hit of all those four cities.

When I got to Houston and looked around, I thought, no way this city's evaporating. It's the fourth-largest city in America. It may be bad and everybody's broke, I get it. But this thing isn't going away, so I'm good to go.

I chose Houston where I found my first 234-unit complex. I'll probably never forget it. I do forget about a lot of them after, because you know, time flies when you're having fun. It's like your first child, right? It's my first "child" in America and it's an unbelievable situation. So, I'll just give you a little detail just to give you a little flavor of what is going on.

The property was in a very nice area. There was a first and second lienholder, and an owner. The lienholder had foreclosed on the owner. The owner paid over $9 million dollars for the complex. The first lien was about $2.5 million, and the second lien was

$3.2 million. The owner had put in the difference in cash so they lost a fortune.

I look at it; I tie it up; and I go, "Okay, now we need to talk." So, I tied it up, because the second lienholder owns it, and I tie it up from them. I say, "Can you get information to contact the first lienholder?" They say absolutely, so I go talk to the first lienholder. Because the second lienholder is a bank and the bank is making the monthly payments to the first lienholder, the first lienholder is totally unaware of the property condition.

I call and say, "Guys, I'm not sure if you know what's going on, but your property is only 50 percent occupied. Every roof in the building leaks and there's not enough money coming in to cover operating expenses. The only reason you're getting paid is because the second lienholder is a bank." Their response was a very somber, 'Oh.'"

I sent them pictures, and then they said, "Oh, s@#t." Now, the second lienholder, his papers were $3.2 million, and he agrees to sell to me. I'm going off memory now, but I think I paid him just $200,000 for his $3.2 million lien and he was just happy to get the monkey off his back–remember, he's making payments every month.

The first lienholder says, "Okay, why the hell should I sell it to you? Or do a deal with you?" I said, "Because I'm going to put a million dollars into this property. I'm going to fix it up, and I'm going to get the value up again."

He asks, "Oh, yeah?" I say, "Absolutely." He then asks, "And would you put the million dollars in escrow?" I responded, "Absolutely, to be used to renovate the property." Then I said, "But I want your note to go out for 10 more years. I want a moratorium on the interest and no principal payments for the first three years. I'm not making any payments. After that, we'll do a sliding scale, two percent a year, three percent a year, but interest only. I'm not giving you any principal." And he agreed!

That all wasn't done in five minutes, you know. It took a while for them to swallow it, but they did the smart thing because their collateral and asset was going down fast.

You have to make an intelligent decision at a certain point in your life. So, I got into that deal, and that was the end of '87. I spent all of '88 bringing the buildings up to snuff. And, as they were coming back online and starting to look good, the market started coming back.

Now, that was just pure luck on my part. But at that time, I had money, and my competition had no money. This "no money" thing went on—even though the market was coming back, the "no money" thing went on for years after I bought that property. So, I got really ahead of my competition. At one point, I was up to around owning 4,000 units. It was almost like taking candy from a kid in a candy store.

For this property, in my second year, my cash flow was at $70,000 a month. That's how much cash I was putting into my pockets. Yes, I still had my million bucks invested, but still, it's $70,000 per month—that's a hell of a return!

But there were times it wasn't easy. I was buying depressed properties in a depressed market—not only in a depressed market, the market wasn't coming back, and you didn't know when it was coming back. During my renovations, I was dumping money in and nobody was coming to lease. It did not feel good. I did have concerns, but that's the way it goes, right?

If it came easy, everybody would be doing it. You've got to have a stomach for it, the desire for it; it's just not that simple. So, I got lucky, and I kept acquiring. I got up to about 4,000 units, and financing started to come back, because there was no financing when I came to the market. None. Zero. No one was lending in Texas, you need to understand that.

Maybe if you go back to the last recession we were in, you'd get a bit of understanding of no money, but there was hard money then. You know, when I was here, there was no hard money. That's the difference. Which was good news for me, because hard money costs money when you're negotiating with a lender who's in trouble.

So, to fast-forward a little bit, the market started coming back. We hit the Gulf War in '92, '93, and things slowed down a little bit. And in '94, '95, the CMBS market—if you don't know what that is, that is a commercial mortgage-backed securities.

Wall Street started creating the bonds again and making loans again, and it was starting to get frothy. I started financing and all that stuff. Then, pretty much the multi-family dried-up and the party was officially over.

And I started getting into office buildings, because they lagged behind the recovery. So, the first thing to come back was multi-family and probably homes. But then I think homes kind of lagged behind also. After that office space came back, so I did some office deals, some hotel deals, and parking-garage deals. Then I decided to sell all my apartments at the same time. I sold them to one buyer for around $90 to $100 million, somewhere in that range.

I sold them to a nonprofit group, and there were a lot of benefits attached to that sale. I stayed on managing for them, because they weren't managers. Then, during the recession, they started to lose them.

It became impossible to keep them occupied. If you remember the timeframe of 2006–2008, the homes were sucking the life out of multi-family. I got out the market at the end of 2003 because I saw the writing on the wall and said, "I'm cashing out, but if you want me to stay on and manage them, I will." I had a team anyway, so I went on to other things, and as I went down my path.

I'll tell you a very interesting story. It's a lot of more interesting today for me, because it's in the past, but when I had to go through it, but it was a life-changing experience for me.

One of the lenders on a property that I had sold hired a fantastic attorney. This guy was great. Up until then, I couldn't say I had any lawsuits that I really filed or that were filed against me. I ran a pretty tight ship. If you know anything about Canadians, you know that they're not contentious; culturally speaking, we don't sue. Of course, here, the culture's a little different. No problem. I'm okay with that. You know, when in Rome, do what the Romans do.

This guy just created a case against me personally. He came up with theories that were way over my head. Then he sues me, so I had to hire an attorney. I'll make a long story short... they ended up getting a judgment against me for 8 million bucks! So, of course, I'm like, "Oh, s@#t!"

I got an attorney that was referred to me. He was good, but again, it's my first foray into lawsuits. I wasn't as experienced as I am today. Don't try me today. But then I had to learn, and learn quickly. I'm not sure how well he's doing, right? I get a phone call one day from his secretary, or paralegal, "Bob just died!" I said, "What?" Bob's my age, and Bob just died. Bob just died. I'll spare you all the details, but he died. Once again, I'm like, "Oh, s@#t, what do I do now?" I've got an $8 million judgment and no attorney.

I made a phone call to someone who I had a lot of respect for and told him my story. He's a forensic accountant. I said, "Look, I need your help. This is what you do all day long, and you work for the best attorneys in town. I need the best." He gave me three names and I interviewed all three. I spent 10 minutes with the third guy, and I hired him. I knew right away, this is a winner. And what a history he had. I give him the case, and fast forward, he blows out the judgment, and sues them for $3 million!

We're talking about a five-year period. Lawsuits don't get fixed overnight. They take three to five years, and I must have added 50 pounds in that five years. Mostly because I had to eat a hell of a lot more, because I had more diarrhea than ever. But you know, it was about a five-year ordeal, and they owed me. It was a hell of a fight; it was extremely stressful. I had more hurdles put in front of me than ever before in my life, in areas I knew nothing about: Law. And I came out the other end. So, if I had to do it all over again, I wouldn't want to. But then, I think the moral of the story is that nothing comes easy. As good as you are, and as much as you learn, and as hard as you try not to get into trouble, plain and simple, it's going to happen.

That's when you separate the men from the boys. You find out if you're the guy that falls down and stays down or the guy that gets up and says, "F#@k you, I'm getting out of it." And so, I'm that kind of guy. I don't always know what my next move is going to be or what it needs to be, and I don't always know enough to know when I'm going to get out of it. But I know enough that once you put me into a corner, I'm not staying there. I'll figure out how to get out, and I'll figure out how to come back. And that's really one thing that everyone has to take with them in life, be prepared to reinvent yourself.

BE PREPARED TO
REINVENT YOURSELF

Reinventing yourself doesn't mean you're going to go from real estate to another industry. You could spend your entire life in this game and make a lot of money and have good times and bad times and trials and tribulations. But within the business, be prepared to reinvent yourself and to remain flexible.

I'm a 65-year-old guy. When I sit down with a 25- or 30- or 40-year-old guy who's in the business, I pay as much attention to this guy as I do to my peers. Why? Because you never know who's going to teach you your next lesson. That's something that I really feel is important for you to keep in the back of your mind.

Nobody knows it all. No matter how long you've been doing it, you keep learning. Be prepared to fight like hell.

Fast-forward to 2010–2012 and the world starts to change again, right? We go through 2008 and 2009, and things are bad. And I'm holding on to my real estate. I've got some pieces that are taking care of themselves. I've got some pieces that need nurturing. I have this hotel that I've built and own - and still own. Hotels are the first to come back and the first to go down because the customers have no long-term contract at hotels. If people stop coming, they stop coming! So, I had to get in there in 2009. In 2008, we had the best year ever, because of the hurricane and the number of people who stayed in hotels because they lost their homes.

In 2009, I think I made 50,000 bucks and broke even and the only reason I broke even was because I went in there and just sliced and diced. I did the stuff that everyone hates doing, which is letting people go and asking one person to do the jobs of four people. It's unpleasant; it's awful; it's terrible, but it's you or them at that point. We just have to do things like that at certain times and it's not just you. The people that stay with you that you could afford to keep, it's for them too. They're staying with you. They're staying employed, but you've got to do what you've got to do.

I guess I'm kind of happy to say that I did not lose any properties during that period. I hung in, and you've got to hang in. The one nice thing about real estate that anyone will tell you if they have been in it long enough is that five to ten years later, you are coming out with a pile of dough, even if you f#@ked up when you bought it wrong in the first place.

Time—it's usually not four to five years. I like to say ten years. Ten years, maybe five, usually cures all wounds and you're starting to see daylight if it gets really bad. Hanging in is important, but knowing when to cut your losses is also important. Knowing when to sell is even more important. This s@#t about "If I keep it forever," I don't believe in it. You have to know when the top of the market is for that property, and that's when you sell.

I have owned some of the same pieces of real estate for 20 years already, and I don't regret it, because they are incredible pieces of real estate. However, I would sell in a heartbeat for the right price. Things started to come back in the market around 2011 and 2012, and by 2012, I started to realize that's it was time to start selling again. Everybody was building and a lot of people were building, and everybody was telling me this building boom is "never going to end" and we've got at least a 20-year run like this.

As soon as I started hearing that, I knew it's time to start selling. My response was, "OK, great! Everybody's happy. Everybody's thinking it's never going to change. Great, then I'm going to sell."

I sold the office building that I had built in 1999. When I sold in 2012, I made out like a bandit. I came back in as a limited partner into the new entity. Today, that property is losing money. It lost a tenant that occupied one-third of the building when oil collapsed, and they're struggling. I got out at the peak. The guys that are in the deal are deep-pocketed and very experienced guys. I am managing it. I know that they back up their financial obligations. I know that they will get through this downturn, but it's not going to be fun. And I don't know when it is going to be worth the price that I sold it to them for back in 2012. It could be another 10 years. It truly does not bother me, because I am in a management role now.

This building is 120,000 square feet, and it's in the energy corridor of Houston, which is a very desirable area to be in, but as we all know, s@#t happens and oil has tanked recently. Look, that's the first time I've ever had a major tenant vacancy in that building, quite frankly, and I've kept it full for 15 years. But nothing goes on forever.

I sold my parking garage around that time, and I also sold another hotel that I owned downtown. When people have to have it, I am happy to sell it, but there's a right time for everything. Then, about two and a half years ago, I decided to reinvent myself. I didn't want to do what I had done for 45 years anymore. I have a lot of respect for guys like you that are doing this business, but I just do not want to do it anymore. I don't care about the upside; I just want the yield. I decided to take my money and do private lending, which I'm very familiar with, because I did a lot of business with private lenders as a borrower.

Private lending was in fashion. When the deal made sense, it didn't matter how much I paid my private lender. It was cheaper than partners, and even if I had some partners, it was still the best financing path I had found to get deals closed.

As an investor, I've always been disciplined. When deals would come to me, if it wasn't an out-of-the-park deal, I would walk away. Like

I said, I'm very disciplined. I don't care; I don't need it. And that has been my attitude with my private lending too.

I love the lending business, because I love to meet people and I love to analyze deals. I don't care how much time I spend in a day looking at a borrower's deal, and if it doesn't happen my way, I'm still smiling. I got to meet him; I got to see the property; I got to see the budget; and I am happy. I'm as happy as a lark.

I believe we all have to have this attitude in our daily business life, which is to walk away if it is not perfect. Just walk away and let the next guy pay more. It doesn't matter. Tomorrow, you'll get another phone call, and the day after, you'll get three more phone calls. My phone doesn't stop ringing.

If I have to see 12 deals before I get one, so what? But the one I get, for me, is a home run. And I go to sleep, and I know where you are. For me, that is extremely important, and I've had that attitude all my life, not just as a private lender.

If a deal didn't make sense, my emotions have never gotten away from me. I don't give a s@#t how pretty it looks or how great it could be, if the numbers did not work my way and I did not feel I had my downside covered and somebody stepped up to the plate and paid more—good luck!

And two or three years later, they either proved me wrong or they proved me right. If they proved me wrong, so what? It doesn't change the way I do business. If they prove me right, okay? It doesn't matter. It's business. It's always just business, and having good relationships with people is what matters most. Even when the chips are down, you should always work to create and maintain a great relationship. It will always come back to you.

You don't have to be mean while doing business. You can be nice and do business. I think it is better to be nice in business, I think, than having people saying behind your back, or even to your face, what a piece of s@#t you are. That isn't fun.

I think if you watch the show *Shark Tank*, which I know I do, who would you like to be on that show? Probably Robert Herjavec, on the right, because he is nice. He is rich, but he's nice. He cares about people. I will tell you that I do like Mark Cuban, for sure. He's not only a shark, but he's a f#@king genius.

He knows what he doesn't know, which is another thing I want to share with you guys.

I landed in Houston from LA, about 6:00 p.m. last night and I got a phone call from a borrower. He's got a food business that he wants to borrow money for. To make a long story short, I called him back and said, it all sounds great, but I know what I don't know, and I know I do not know the food business. So, even though I know I can write you a check, that is not all you need. You need help. You need guidance, and I cannot give you that. Also, because I don't know your business, I am likely going to lose money on it. So, when you start to make money, don't let that money start to fool you. You do not know anything else. By the time you know this business, you will be at least 10 years older, and maybe 20 years older. Correct me if I am wrong, but that's my experience. It takes 10 years to be able to be somewhat of an expert, and 20 years probably to make some serious money. And if you are not smart enough, you'll lose it all.

I had a lot of meetings this week in Los Angeles, and we talked about how you can never change your principles and you have to stick to what you know.

The last thing I can think of that I want to share with you is that when I get up every day, I don't feel like I am working. I am excited just to get up, go run seven miles, and then go look for the next deal! It's a great life, but I'm 65, and it took me a long time to get here. I wish it happened to me 20 years ago, but I was too busy making money, doing it differently. But what's done is done, and I don't regret it. You've just got to build it, and it takes time. You've got to clean the toilet before you can move up the ladder.

I've shared everything that I can think of, but if you guys have some questions, I'll try my best to give you some good answers.

[Question from the group]

What do you look for when a borrower approaches you?

The first thing I look for is does the borrower know what they're doing? I come across a lot of people that really don't know what they are doing. If they do not know what they are doing, I cannot help them, because I'm not going to do all of the work. The second thing I look for is if they know what they're doing, that means they passed the first test, and by the way, it's easy for me to know if they know what they're doing. I will also mention that I don't care if they don't know what they're doing if they have someone with them who knows, and then I'm good.

If they are willing to learn, let me introduce them to someone I know who knows what they are doing to partner with them, then I'm happy to do that. But, on their own, I am not willing to be their lender if they don't know what they're doing.

Next, location is extremely important. The condition of the home – I don't care how bad it is. I will walk inside and out. I want to know what you're going to do. I want to agree with what you're going to do. I am not going to tell you what to do. I am going to suggest, "Hey, maybe you should put carpet here. Maybe you should put hardwoods here," and suggestions like that. I am going to say those types of things, and you should probably listen to me, because if I'm saying it, I guarantee you it's coming from experiences I've had somewhere from some point in time. Also, when I'm the lender, the benefits for all to go well are aligned for me and the borrower, so I'm going to offer my input and do my due diligence on values.

I will tell you that I don't do appraisals like most lenders. I do it myself. I remain very conservative, of course. I will look at comps. I will call a local realtor in the area, and from the time I see the house or the property, within 24 or 48 hours, I will make an offer on my lending terms.

[Question from the group]

I'm in the Dallas/Ft. Worth market, and there seems to be a ridiculous amount of multi-family property being built. It looks as if they are just building them everywhere. Would that still be a market you would recommend getting into?

From an investment point of view, I love Dallas. I haven't done a deal in Dallas yet, but I've done some in Austin. But I'm dying to do some deals in Dallas. I've seen a few, but I've walked away.

They weren't multi-family deals; they just weren't deals that I felt comfortable doing. I think Dallas is in a better space today than Houston. That doesn't make Houston bad; it just makes Houston more competitive. You have to be a lot smarter here today because of the oil thing. Dallas seems to have avoided a good part this oil problem, correct me if I am wrong.

I think you're correct. I saw a report that showed the amount of office space in Dallas currently occupied by companies in the energy industry was only around 15 percent versus Houston, which was in the 80 percent range. The amount of oil companies that are using office space based in Houston is significantly more than oil companies in Dallas.

Huge things are going on in Dallas, and I love it. There's nothing wrong with looking at multi-family.

They are building a lot of multi-family everywhere right now, and I think that certain markets, like Houston, are saturated and overbuilt right now. That is the good and the bad news. Why do I say that? I say that the good news is because I don't own any of it right now. The bad news is that, if you do own it, you may be in serious trouble and you haven't seen anything yet. I can spend an hour on that, but that's going to create opportunity, and I'm a lender. And when the time is right, maybe in a year or two, I'll be doing multi-family loans, and I would also do them today, but of course, it depends where and what size and how much money.

There are certain pockets in Houston that are great for multi-family. If you go to the east side of town, where the refineries and chemical plants are blowing and going, and they're expanding them, they're spending billions. I would look at multi-family, even single-family and even retail, as a value-add opportunity. I think that's a very good place to invest in the Houston market. But I'm looking for home-run deals, because for the rest of the Houston market, and other markets, there's a lot more pain to come. I will even give you my crystal-ball projection that says, here's what is going to happen.

We are likely going to see history repeat itself. The new multi-family apartments that are Class A are offering three months' free rent right now. You know what that means to pro-formas, right? Shut down. Once they're leased up, if they're not a pension fund, they may be done. Game over. With pension funds, you feel the pain, but they're all cash. No leverage, no problem. You're not happy, but you get through.

The guy with the leverage, right, there are a lot of guys out there with leverage, and I know, they borrowed their money cheap—four percent, five percent maybe? But here's the problem: That money is going to become expensive now, because your NOI is down by a quarter. At the end of your construction loan term, your lender expects you to take them out of the loan, because it's not long-term.

He's a short-term construction lender, not long-term, so he wants his money back. He underwrites your deals, and he's now asking the question, "How are you going to take me out of this loan?" Your values are shot to hell, and you're upside down. You can't get a loan big enough to take me out now. You know, maybe your deal was supposed to be worth $50 million. Now it's worth $35 million. And you know what? I think that's what you owe me. So ya know what? I think you need to write me a check for 10 million, then go look for financing to take me out of this loan. These guys can't write checks for $10 million. If they could write checks for $10 million, they wouldn't even need the money in the first place.

The other thing that happens is the people that were living in a Class C apartment can now afford a Class A apartment because of the Class A discounts the owners are giving. Now what happens to the people living in the Class Bs and Cs? So, it's a trickle-down effect. Trickle up, trickle down. Or trickle down and trickle up, however you want to look at it or say it. I lived through this cycle and I've seen that the opportunities are in all classes, because one day, it's going to come back.

You know, when I was here buying 4,000 units, I was buying Bs and Cs. There was another genius who came to town, who only bought the A classes and I thought he was making a mistake only buying the As. As it turned out, he made off like a bandit as well. When it comes back, it comes back across the board. So, when his values went up, my values went up; everybody goes up together. Everybody goes down together; everybody goes up together. The guy that's unleveraged doesn't have to lose his property. The guys that are leveraging and don't have the cash reserves, well, they're going to bleed. That's where you're going and it's not going to change. I don't care what price oil goes to this year. If it gets to 60 bucks at the end of the year, they're still in trouble. The damage is done because, once again, everything lags behind. So, if you've got oil companies blowing their brains out right now—right? By the time they are starting to make money, do you think they are going to start bringing everybody back online right away? No. Do you think they are going to increase their budgets and spend billions again right away? No. There's a period of time where they just sit and recover, right?

[Question from the group]
And that's when we need to be rushing in?

Yes, you have to watch them. You don't want to get in too early and now is too early. Unless you're going out to the east side of town, then we can go on the east side all day long. But it better be fast, because I think you have a two-year window. I like Dallas. I like all asset classes in Dallas. Again, you have to watch closer with multi-family, because everywhere in the country they're getting to a point where they are probably building too many. They are overbuilt. Now, it's like Houston in the crash of the eighties. Houston fell a lot farther than Dallas and Austin. Dallas held up better. Dallas is a good place to be now.

[Question from the group]
You think it is just more because of the diversity of industries (in Houston)?

It is, and was then, and it is even more so now. There's a lot going on in Dallas.

[Question from the group]
What type of asset classes will you lend on as a private lender?

Single-family, hotel, office, multi-family, industrial, and parking.
What do you want?

[Question from the group]

Do you have a minimum in terms of dollar amount?

A couple weeks ago, I turned a guy down for a $20,000 loan.

I have done loans as low as $65,000 and as high as $1.4 million, and I'll go much higher. We'll lend on deals in the millions.

[Question from the group]

On a single-family home, what are your typical lending terms?

I am more expensive than some people in this room would tell you. That's not necessarily a good thing for me. I understand that. But it's the truth. You can call Brant, and he will get you a much better deal than I'm prepared to do, most likely. There's a lot of competition today in private lending, as you know.

Guys like me are having a tougher time. Of course, again, I don't need to do the deals. I want to do the deals, but I need to love the deal before I do it.

[Question from the group]

Will you lend if the borrower plans on having a second lien or multiple liens?

I love second liens coming after me. It means there is another party interested in wanting this deal to go the right way. Right? So, more people with skin in the game is a good thing. For me, I want skin in the game. And if you're not putting skin in the game somehow, I won't do the deal.

[Question from the group]

So, tell us an ideal scenario for a deal that you would say yes to right away.

I'll be happy to do that. An ideal scenario would be no more than 65% of the value I come up with, right?

I want an experienced borrower or a borrower that has someone like Brant here that I would support any deal that he is in. I want to know when I'm dealing with people that they know what they're doing or have someone on their team that knows.

I believe in giving at least a one-year term. The reason for that is because s@#t happens. I see a lot of those less-expensive lenders out there doing six-month terms, cheaper than me. But, for the cost of the money to roll into the next six months, then you get a little more f#@ked.

What I'm really concerned about with those kinds of deals is what if they don't want to extend it after the first six months? That's always kind of bothered me as a lender. So, I say to my borrower, "I am giving you a year, and it's not costing you anything to take the year, but this way, trust me, s@#t happens." And so, he gets a year. I usually like to ask for a minimum yield of five to six months on my money. So, if you get really lucky, you're ready to pay me off in three months, which is really lucky. It's not typical, right? I've had it happen where I've gotten paid off quickly in just a couple of months, but not often.

I make at least a five- or six-month yield depending on the situation, because my attitude is, I don't charge to come visit. I don't charge for my analysis or time. There are no fees with me. No upfront fees...

Sure, I charge points if I do the deal, but at first, if we don't do a deal that you send to us, it doesn't cost you anything. If we do our deal, I'm not charging you processing fees and handling fees and this fee and that fee, plus points. I don't do that. Whenever my lawyer charges five-, six-, or seven-hundred bucks, you'll pay him at closing. Whatever we negotiate in interest and points, you pay me, and that's it.

[Question from the group]
Can you give us a range of what you typically get on interests and points?

I get 12 to 18 percent, plus or minus points. I've done some deals at 12 percent, but I've charged a couple of points. I've done 18 percent with no points, because I can't go over 18 percent because of usury laws.

I've done everything in between. I figured out my average the other day is about 14.5 percent, annualized, which isn't a bad return. I think it's a great return. In today's market, I know guys are getting a lot less. So. I've gone as low as 12 percent, but it was a sweetheart deal. I do construction loans too.

[Question from the group]

For example, let's use a simple number, like $100,000. If the deal is at 65 percent, you still want the investor to have skin in the game?

Yes. Here's an example of a $100,000 deal I had. A guy buys the house and he pays $100k. He put $30k into the deal to renovate it. He's in the deal for $130k. He figures it's going to sell for about $170k.

I lend him $100k at closing, but also at closing, he gives me $30k to hold, which I fund as he completes the renovations. I want to know that he's got skin in the game, and I want to know that the money's for the rehab, because if he gets run over by a bus the day after closing, what the hell am I going to do? I am going to call Brant. I'm going to say, "Brant, I got 30 grand. You better not spend a dime more. Get this f#@king thing done and sold for $170k!"

[Question from the group]

James, why did you go that way versus just having him put $30k into the purchase of the house?

That's what he accepted. I was okay if he did it that way too, but I was happy to do it this way. First, he agreed to that and that gave me interest on my $100k instead of interest on only $70k. And like I said, he agreed to it. He did a great job, by the way. And he's paying me off on Monday. He sold the house for $170k.

Guys, typically if you are working with a lender who lends with less than a one-year term, it could mean one of two things:

One, it's an inexperienced lender. They may have some nervousness or animosity about loaning, and they don't understand the business, so they want it to be quick. Be wary of that. We, as borrowers, require one-year loans, or we're not going to do the deal with that lender.

Number two, some of the hard-money kind of guys are intentionally doing a six-month loan so they can charge you to renew the loan. I don't want to call it a scam, but it's set up for them to make more money off your inexperience. So just be aware of these things.

[Question from the group]

I have a question, but it's not about how to make money. My question is: How do you manage your money? Do you follow a scale of percentage? Possibly what you live off and what you invest? What have you followed throughout your career that has served you well?

That's a great question. I do have a plan and I've always had a plan, but plans don't always work out the way you plan. I must say that because it happens to everybody. I've got other assets throwing off cash daily. The hotel, for example, and I've got a couple of office buildings. One isn't throwing off any cash, but the other one is. I know I've got income streams there and I do keep a significant amount of cash available so that I don't get caught. Percentage-wise, I can't say that I really have a formula. In my lending business, I'm unleveraged. That's huge for me because I don't have to answer to anyone.

I go wherever I want. If the s@#t hits the fan, who cares? Nobody can spook me if the market goes to hell in a hand basket and I have to start taking back houses, which is the last thing I want to do. I've got to pay taxes, and I've got to pay insurance, but I'm not leveraged. So that's a big advantage. I like to do every "great" deal when it comes my way. But I can't do every deal, because I don't have a bottomless pit, like I explained to my wife this morning as she showed me the beautiful $3,000 purse she just bought. I'm just joking about the purse; I want her to be happy with the purse... But you know, I don't have a bottomless pit, but I like to do every great deal.

So, what I'm starting to consider is to partner with people on my lending, to let others participate to where, if I get to the point where I can say, "Hey, you know what? I want to leave my liquidity the way it is, for whatever reason, I can bring in others." I can still do the deal and stay liquid. But I don't work on percentages. But, again, I have no leverage. I have no debt. Yes, I have debt on my hotel, but it's non-recourse. I have debt on my office buildings, but it's non-recourse. But everything I own is paid for.

Anyway, I know we're getting close to our time, but look, I'm 65; I'm not 35 years old anymore. I don't need a plane. I don't need five houses. I'm past all that s@#t. So, it's a lot different for me than maybe for some of you young guys coming up. I'm just having fun doing what I do, and I don't care how much more I make, but I do want to protect it. My son cares, and he's probably going to build it up much bigger. He's already started to.

[Question from the group]

What's the driving force for you right now? Is it the art of the deal?

I'm in love with the art of the deal, that's what I wake up for. I'm like a junkie. If I go a day without a phone call, which I don't—if I go, let's say, a couple of hours without a phone call, I'm f#@ked up, man. I'm f#@ked up. I start shaking.

I got a call from an Austin guy on a Friday. Saturday morning, I was there. I just got in the car and drove. Look, I've got nothing else to do! That's the other thing too, is that I don't have anything else to do. So, what am I going to do? Sit home and eat chocolate chip cookies? No. Oh, my God. I'll have to run 10 miles a day instead to keep it off. It takes seven miles a day just to keep it like this!

I've lost about 70 pounds. I've kept it all off for three years now by eating healthier and running seven miles a day.

[Question from the group]

What advice do you give to investors who want to find deals and other opportunities (commercial, multi-family, etc.) in other markets or states? What are some of the steps you would you recommend for them to go about finding deals in other markets?

I'll just tell how I did my things. So, again, it was a totally depressed market, so you have to go a lot by your gut. You have to go down there; you have to put your boots on the ground; and you've got to get a feel for the market. How are you going to get a feel from the market? Well, you know, you have to spend a week there. You start to talk to the brokers. You start to meet people. Talk to a guy in a restaurant. Talk to the guy who is driving. Put your boots on the ground, and if you start to feel like this might be a place you want to be, then you are going have to start to understand the way things work in that market. Both in the legal aspect — from taxing, city codes, and permits — and finding all those stones you have to turn over, and just take it from there.

CONCLUSION

Before we go, I want to thank you for reading this book and, more importantly, I hope that this book has inspired you to go out and take action to create results in your life and business. Remember, within these pages lies some of the keys for you to create your own success and wealth through real estate investing.

If you're interested in starting your real estate investing business, or trying to get to the next level with your investments, please contact me and schedule a coaching session so we can discuss the goals and results you're seeking. You can schedule a time for a call and also find many helpful resources by going to BrantPhillips.com/Resources

Lastly, I love hearing success stories. As you go down your own path to creating real estate wealth, if you have gained value and motivation from this book, please reach out to let me know. It means a lot to me.

That's all I've got. Now get out there and start taking action.

All the Best,
Brant

ABOUT BRANT PHILLIPS

Brant is a full-time real estate investor, business owner, business coach, speaker and bestselling author. He has been featured on Fox News as a Real Estate expert and hosts local seminars and training events.

Brant is a proverbial 'rags to riches' story. While living in an apartment and having no money, he was able to purchase his first investment property on a credit card.

Brant went on to buy 10 properties that same year with no money down. Since that time, has gone on to purchase, renovate, flip and rent hundreds of homes. He owns a portfolio of rental properties in the millions and continues to flip houses and take part in a variety of real estate projects, including new home construction and development.

In addition to Brant's real estate pursuits, he's an active entrepreneur as the owner of a coaching and consulting business and a property management company. Brant also owns a marketing company that helps small businesses and entrepreneurs to utilize the same marketing strategies he uses in his businesses. One of Brant's companies, Invest Home Pro, was recognized by Inc. 5000 as one of America's Fastest-Growing Private Companies.

Brant is a former police officer who prides himself on integrity and serving others. He is a husband and father of five and enjoys helping and teaching people to experience the freedom and success he has achieved through successfully investing in real estate.

You can learn more about Brant at BrantPhillips.com